"THE EARLY WORM GETS THE BIRD"

comics & paintings by
damian willcox

special thanks to my very lovely & talented wife miyuki,
and also the 'not a real doctor' "dr." bill(y) wong for all
of the help, feedback and suggestions.

"THE EARLY WORM GETS THE BIRD"

published by dorkboy comics in canada

www.dorkboycomics.com

introduction

i have just realized that as of next year, it will have been twenty years since i penned my first "dorkboy" comic back in college. said comic involved our illustrious hero "dorkboy", nazi warplanes, flying potatoes and heat seeking exploding turtles, and was my intoxicating entry into the world of comics...well, if we are to exclude the "Robobill" comics I had created in grade 8 involving a hybrid of Robocop & SNL's 'Mr. Bill' character, which maybe we should. (though trust me when I tell you that hilarity did indeed ensue upon Robobill's arrival on the scene... for me anyway)

what started out as a quickly sketched comic, while sitting on the hallway floor during lunchtime in college as part of an effort to help supply a friend's publication in need of a filler page ten minutes before a deadline, seems to have grown into an incurable epidemic. oh sure, i had drawn before that..for MANY years before that actually, though primarily in the vein of photo-realism (and sometimes ninjas), but it was missing something...something i found in comics. that thing was levity, it was accessibility, and most of all it was the ability to deliver twisted attempts at humour to a receptive audience from a remote location like some sort of fundamentally broken pizza delivery service that instead delivers bad puns and corny jokes to total strangers anywhere in the world! (and in under 30 minutes or it's free!)

so, i guess what i'm really trying to say is this:

welcome friend, i hope you enjoy my book.

♥damian

"danger? party of one?"

this drawing will also be in the 2014 Calgary Expo Artbook
....and is based on real life of course.
(ink & watercolour)

"hello friend"

this past year saw many travels - this was started on a plane from Shanghai and finished in a hotel in Singapore.
(ink & watercolour)

どもありがと

"domo arigatou"

(pencil & watercolour)

"not your usual quarterback

(ink & watercolour)

"i know bot-fu"

(ink & watercolour)

"these crude instruments"

(manga studio)

"rainbot"

a more refined robot.
i suspect he's on his way
home to put on slippers
and read the paper.
(ink & watercolour)

"aurora bot-realis"

in honour of the beautiful
Northern Lights often visible
near my hometown.
(ink & watercolour)

"monsieur roboto"

i blame these robot/love
themes on learning of the Tin
Man needing a heart in the
Wizard of Oz.
(adobe ideas app)

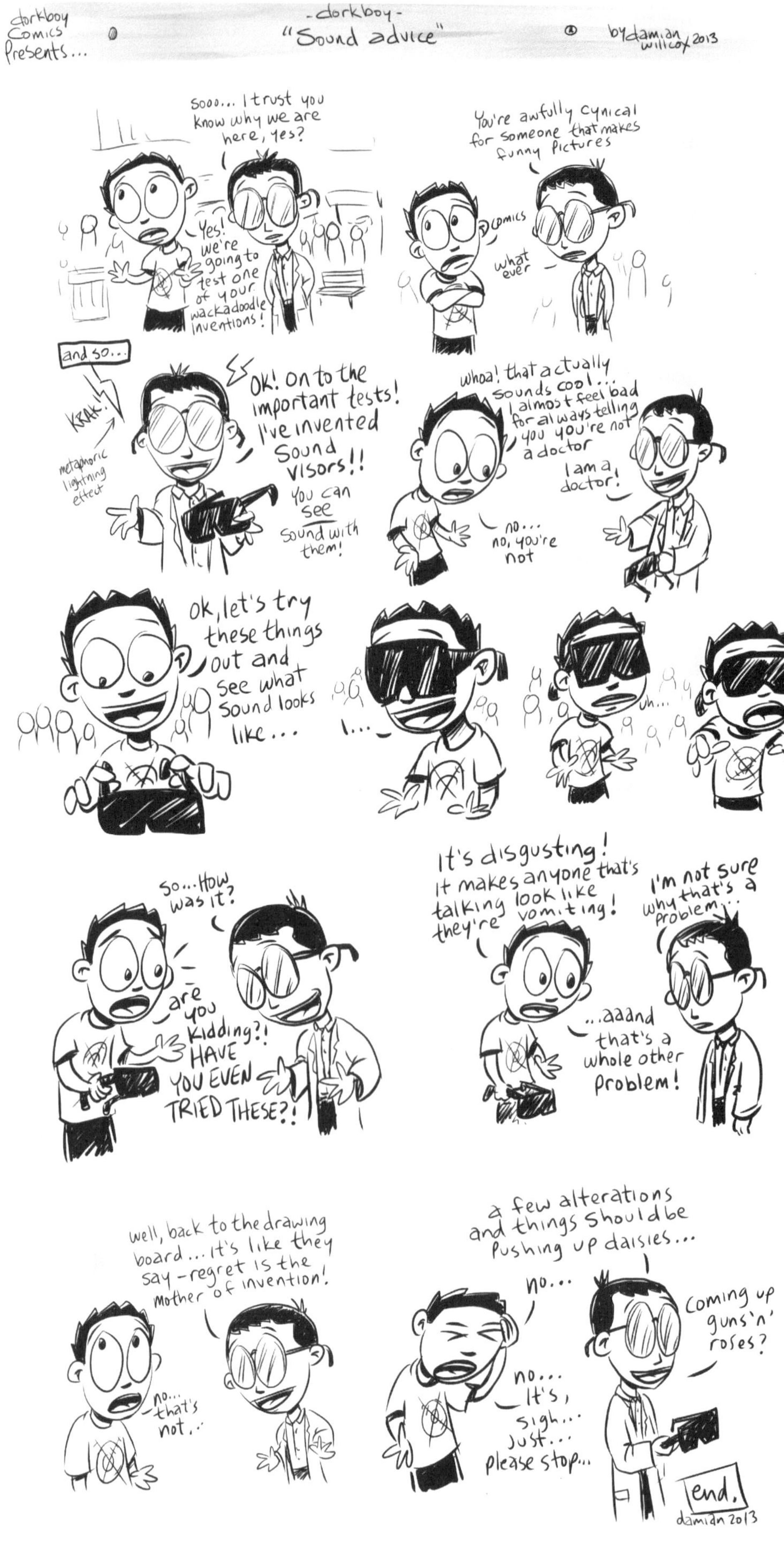

dorkboy Comics Presents...
-dorkboy-
"Sound advice"
by damian willcox 2013
Sooo... I trust you know why we are here, yes?
Yes! we're going to test one of your wackadoodle inventions!
You're awfully cynical for someone that makes funny pictures
comics
what ever
and so...
KRAK!
metaphoric lightning effect
OK! on to the important tests! I've invented Sound visors!! You can see sound with them!
whoa! that actually sounds cool... I almost feel bad for always telling you you're not a doctor
I am a doctor!
no... no, you're not
Ok, let's try these things out and see what sound looks like...
I...
uh...
Yuck!
So... How was it?
are you kidding?! HAVE YOU EVEN TRIED THESE?!
It's disgusting! It makes anyone that's talking look like they're vomiting!
I'm not sure why that's a problem...
...aaand that's a whole other problem!
well, back to the drawing board... It's like they say - regret is the mother of invention!
no... that's not...
a few alterations and things should be pushing up daisies...
no...
Coming up guns'n' roses?
no... It's, sigh... Just... please stop...
end.
damian 2013

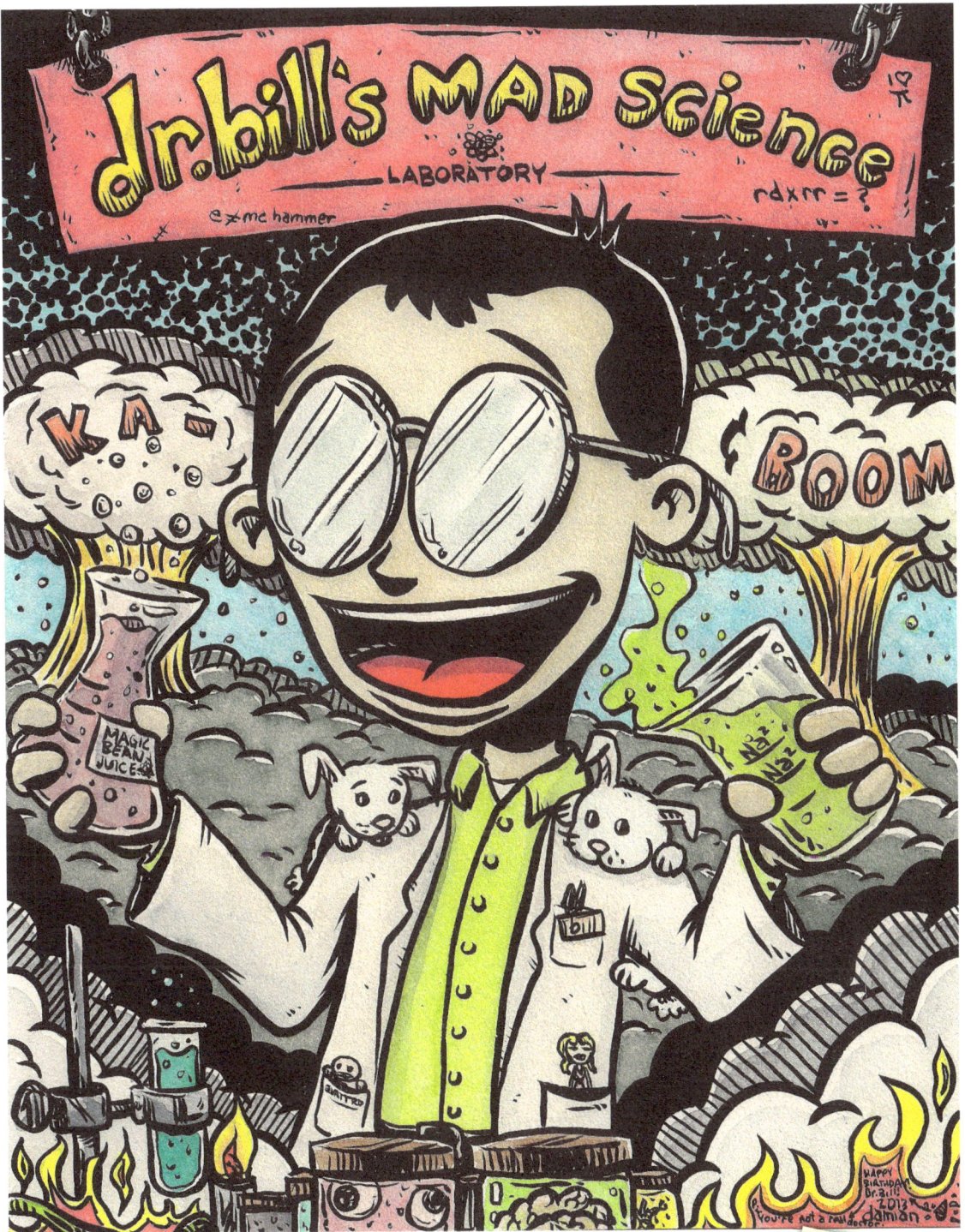

"welcome to the madhouse"

birthday present for the friend that is the basis for
the "dr.bill" character in the dorkboy comics.
original sketch of the idea is on the right.
...and no he's not a real doctor.
(ink & watercolour)

"flotation advice"

by damian willcox

with all of my recent travels, i was thinking about this a LOT. in retrospect, there are probably better things to think about before you fly...

Japan Travelogues

the cartoon below is my very first ever written completely in Japanese!! it also seemed like a fitting intro to the next section which follows my adventures on a recent trip to Japan.

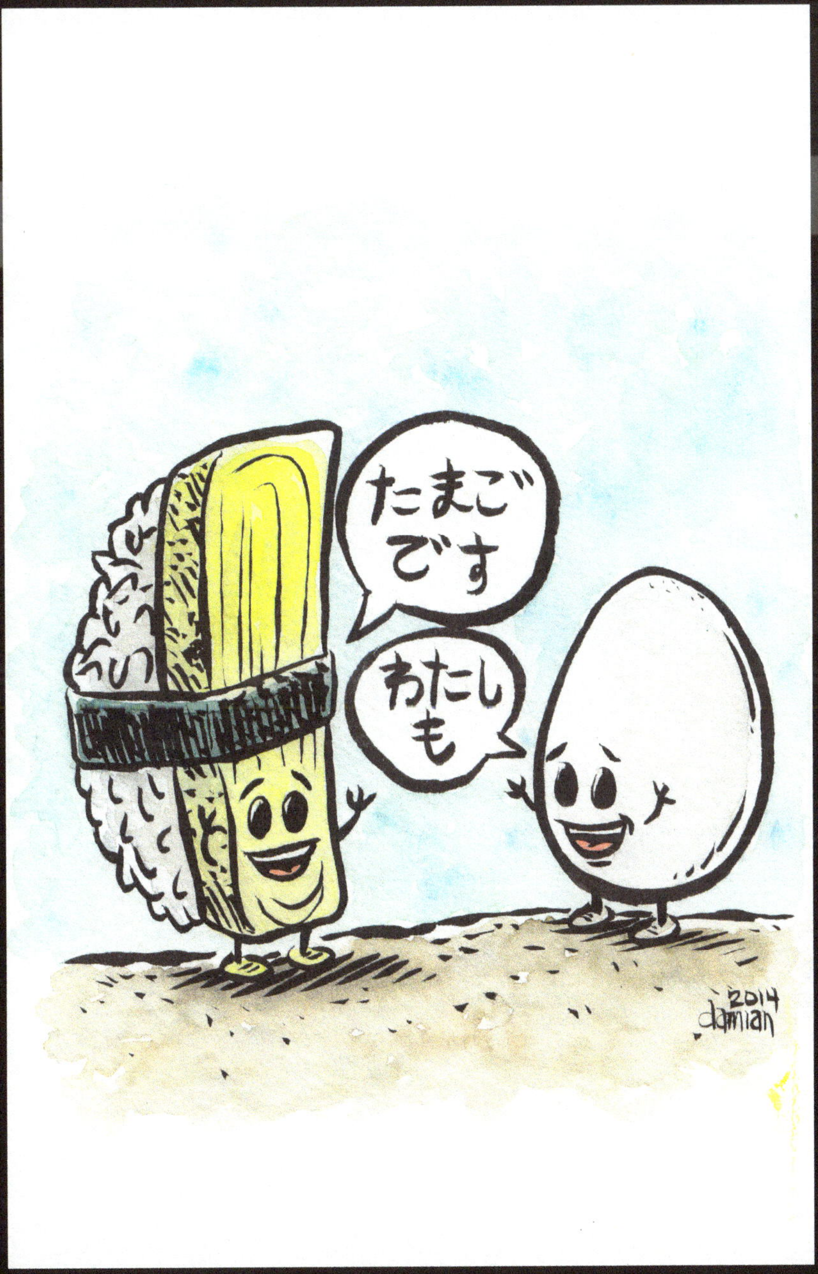
たまごです
わたしも
2014
damian

"tamago desu!" "watashi mo!"

translation: "I'm egg!" "me too!"

Japan Travelogue (one)... by damian willcox 2013

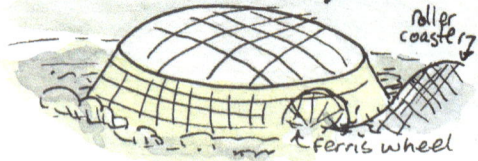

yes i bought a towel...and t-shirt...and key chain. don't judge me.
AND it was the most amazing concert i have ever seen...
AAAND i did get this pic of the stadium before the guy caught me :)

JAPAN TRAVELOGUE (No. 2) . . . . by damian willcox 2013

now to explain the wacky & wonderful world of Japanese toilets

Pronounced oh-toy-uh-ray in Japanese

My mom-in-law's toilet opens the lid as you approach!! like a robot!

feed me seymour!*

*'Little Shop of Horrors' reference

There are also an array of buttons on Japanese toilets...

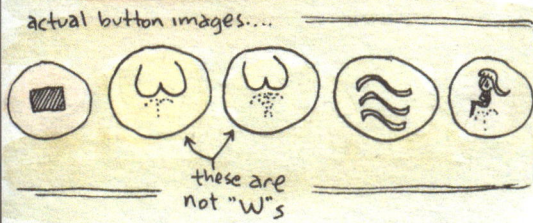

actual button images....

these are not "W"s

though most of them cause liquids to shoot up your butt at varying speeds + temperatures

←trauma shakes

and then there's the bath!

"IANIE"

NSFW

I start out washing in a little room with a drain & showerhead...it's cold in winter here!

my breath, not steam

←brr, it's winter

drain

...and then fit myself into the bath

hmm...maybe if I fold myself...

(me)

(nsfw)

6'-1"

3'-0"   3'-6"

3'-0"

(metal bath box)

TA-DAH!

rollup cover to keep heat from escaping (and me)

x-ray

stay tuned for more!

damian 2013

i hope i haven't frightened you off, Japanese toilets are actually wonderful! you should definitely try them out if you visit...not that you'll have a choice, really.

Welcome to 2014!! YEAR OF THE HORSE!

why the long face?

I'm a horse...

neigh neigh

In Japan, there are a few key elements of New Year's

kimono in winter, Yukatta in summer

Going to the Temple...

goal

food

food

food

...but in order to get there you must pass a Million kiosks selling delicious food like chocolate covered bananas as well as more acquired tastes like Octopus tentacles

Sticky rice cake of doom

...and then there's Sticky rice cakes

PEOPLE DIE EVERY New Year's choking on these traditional treats!

I KILL TOO!

Fugu

CRAZY NEW YEAR'S SALES.

SALE

SALE 80

JAN 60%

EVERY STORE HAS A NEW YEAR'S SALE, SO THEY ARE ALL COMPETING FOR YOUR ATTENTION. THIS IS A TECHNIQUE CALLED "STANDING ON A LADDER WITH A BIG SIGN AND YELLING AT PEOPLE" THAT IS EMPLOYED QUITE FREQUENTLY...

BUY STUFF NOW! RAWR!!

SALE 70

AND TIME WITH FAMILY, which inevitably Includes wacky Japanese TV shows...

Kotatsu (heated coffee table)

I could dedicate a whole comic to Japanese TV, but a lot of shows follow the "variety show" format from the 1970's where, from what I can see, celebrities must taste a lot of different foods...after this, they need to FREAK OUT over how good it tastes...

OMG! OH-EE-SHEE!! EEEEKI!! OO-MAI!!

BEST TASTE EVER!

TOO MUCH LOTS OF on screen Graphics + Animation

more adventures soon.

2014 damian

new year's in japan is a really nice time to see family, and try so many delicious foods....omg so much food. did i mention the food?

today we visited Enoshima on the east coast of Japan!

ENOSHIMA

Being Canadian, I was interested to find out that ENOSHIMA's sister city is Windsor, Ontario!

the plaque described Windsor as being near Detroit and having casinos that were becoming Popular in recent years

THERE WAS A SMALL COBBLESTONE ROAD THERE LINED WITH SMALL SHOPS ...ONE ADVERTISED "DR. FISH", FOOT CLEANER

who is this magical doctor fish?

Dr. Fish!

¥500

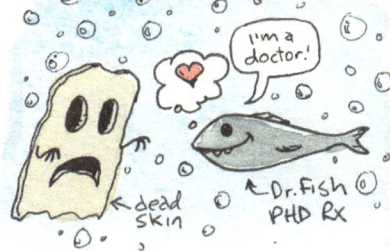

"Dr. Fish" turned out to be a whole bunch of 'piranha' 'like' fish that apparently love to eat dead skin...

I'm a doctor!

dead skin

Dr. Fish PHD Rx

FOR 500 YEN, YOU get to soak your feet in a tub filled with TONS of these hungry fishies that instantly target your SOLE!

like heat seeking missiles

chew
chew
eat
bite
chew
eat
SWARM!!

(bad) pun
cue ominous music

If you don't look & try to forget that there are a LOT of little fishes eating you, it feels kind of like putting your foot on a Jacuzzi jet in a tub

sink to wash feet before

feet go in here

wow! they're soft now!

fish tank

walking back, afterwards...

my feet are still tingling!!

... I hope there aren't any little fish trapped between my toes!*

* there weren't

THE NIGHT ENDED WITH THE DISCOVERY OF WHY MY MOM-IN-LAW'S DOG HAD SUCH BAD BREATH...

Yuck! did you just eat your poop?!!

doggie bag

yum

stay tuned for more!

2014 damian

this was the scariest, strangest, most wonderful experience ever...and apparently quite common, there are other places that have much larger fish that do the job...shudder.

this was my second time sketching with old & new friends in tokyo, and is without fail such a fun time - thanks everyone for letting this crazy canadian tag along!

my cartoon of the sketching friends - in a manga office!

WORK: [しごと]
1. DRAW
2. DRAW
3. DRAW
4. DRAW

what i drew from the ferris wheel....

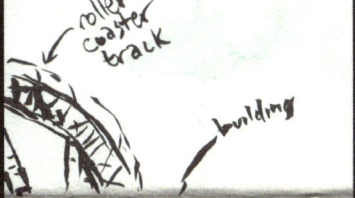

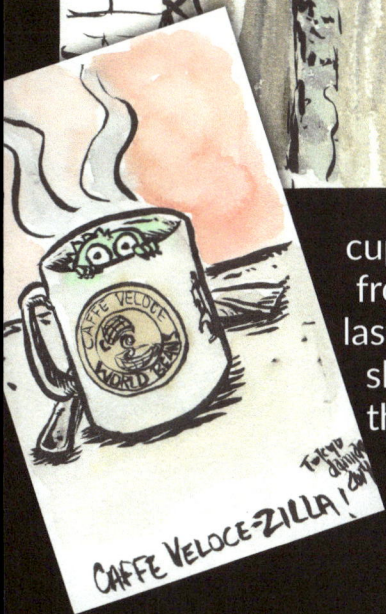

roller coaster track

building

TRAIN TRACK

cup o zilla from the last coffee shop of the day

CAFFE VELOCE-ZILLA!

Tokyodome City
(before we got kicked out)

17

hang on to your Onigiri* folks! it's time to talk about Japanese Convenience Stores or "Konbini"

*dramatic effect

ONIGIRI: Rice ball with stuff inside + seaweed outside

Japan has almost double the number of 7-11's as the U.S., and 7-11 Japan controls all 7-11s in the world!

I'm in Konbini heaven!

SPEAKING OF 7-11...

on this trip we visited Hokkaido* and our hotel room was 711!!!

I sense a flash back coming on...

over 10 years ago...

WHOA!! 711?! IT'S AN OMEN!

I thought you were an omen* "damian"?

Just married

*old movie reference

*future travelogue

anyways... Focus!! Konbinis are filled with deliciousness...

SNACKS

hungry canadian >

Look at this thing!!

WARM BOTTLED + CANNED DRINKS ARE KEPT IN A "HOT FRIDGE"

2 PANCAKES FUSED TOGETHER WITH MAPLE SYRUP + BUTTER INSIDE!!

KIRIN

orange cap on 'hot' drinks

MILK TEA

COFFEE BOSS

HOTTO! HOTTO!

...and they have healthy meals!!

sushi rolls with seaweed packed separately to keep it fresh!

Steamed buns filled with AWESOME!

 < natto

OMURICE!*

*omurice: omelette over rice with sauce

So after all this great food, what next? stay tuned for the adventure of throwing out garbage in Japan!!

damian 2014

the background pic shows part of the 'hot ginger ale' can from the konbini - made by Canada Dry apparently! i can only hope the hot soft drinks revolution catches on here one day.

18

familyMart

So you're in Japan, and you just ate some oishii* onigiri** from the konbini and need to throw out some gomi (garbage) ...easy, right?

*delicious
**←last episode

gomi

WRONG!

here we have a standard garbage can in North America...

...and here is one in Japan!

AGHH!!

toss
bounce

8 million different compartments

didn't study for this test!

but fear not!! you just need to ask yourself a few simple questions first! ...are you throwing out a can or a bottle?

can?

...and if it's a bottle, is it a regular bottle or a PET bottle?

regular bottle
good boy
ruff!
PET bottle
PET

Ok, none of those? There are still more categories... how do you think the garbage will **BURN?** maybe it can go into the "combustible" bin? oh no? how about the "non-combustible" bin?

oh, you have newspaper? it's combustible, yes? but wait!!

NEWSPAPER IS A SEPARATE CATEGORY!!

NEWSPAPER

combustible   non-combustible

AAAAGHH!!! ...or maybe you have gone crazy from so many choices, but good news!! you can still use the "other" bin!!

OTHER   EVERYTHING ELSE   2014 damian

i didn't even mention the household garbage schedule! this involves separating home garbage and putting specific types out on certain days!

19

Japan Travelogue No.8 .... by damian willcox 2014

a trip to Japan is never complete without a visit to the local "Onsen"

'Onsens' are hot baths open to the public - almost like a community 'Rec Centre'

I'm floating!

wait... am I a flotation device?

I can't swim!!

orange you dramatic...

...they quite often fill the baths with special additions... like oranges or rubber duckies

The Onsen in Saitama also has a Shiatsu massage area and a small restaurant... with ice cream!

menu with pictures

doorbell to call waitress

I even drew one of the travelogues here!!

TATAMI MAT

They used to have a "no tattoos" sign in Japanese depicting a huge yakuza (mafia) style tattoo

good thing I can't read

THIS HAS BEEN REPLACED WITH ONE IN ENGLISH SHOWING A FOREIGN GIRL WITH A TINY STRAWBERRY TATTOO...

NO!!! TATTOO!

IF WE FIND ONE WE WILL ASK YOU TO LEAVE!!

IT'S KIND OF FUNNY BECAUSE THESE SIGNS ARE MEANT TO KEEP OUT TROUBLESOME MAFIA TYPES... I'M PRETTY SURE THEY'RE NOT WORRIED ABOUT WHITE GIRLS WITH FRUIT TATTOOS...

black sedan

YAKUZA not fruit

I KNOOOOW!! LIKE OMG! RIIIGHHTT?? THAT IS SOOO CRAYZAY!! WHATEVS!! I'M SOOOO OVER IT!!

fruit

...um... of course, I have been known to be wrong...

こちいよ!! EEYAH!

help!

2014 damian

the local onsen's new and very expanded list of prohibitions is shown in the background here - i managed to sneak in a few times before, but it's getting trickier! they're on to me!

another big plus of using suica is that it makes you look less like a tourist, and there is a LOT less fumbling through change trying to figure out the different coins if you are new to the currency.

so, on this trip to Japan, I noticed my mom-in-law wearing a red sweater with spider web patterns all over it!

← almost like spider-man!!

okaasan
SPIDER WEBS!

...but then I came to my senses. I mean, why would my wife's mom be wearing a spider-man sweater, right?

← crazy talk.

anyway...the reason I've called you here today is to teach you some helpful Japanese!

today we'll learn the word "SUGOI"

'SUGOI' can mean 'good', be used for pleasant surprises or...almost anything really!!

look, a cupcake... AH, SUGOI!!

← for example (...more food coming soon in this comic.)

"THIS IS HOW YOU SAY" I FIND YOUR PEN TO BE OF PLEASANT WORKMANSHIP AND ACCEPTABLE QUALITY, BOB""

Oooh, sugoi!

THIS IS HOW YOU SAY "THE WHIPPED CREAM ON THIS SPECIALTY COFFEE IS SURPRISINGLY BEAUTIFUL AND CLOUD LIKE"

SPEAK SLOWLY FOR EMPHASIS

SSSSUUUU GOI!!

SPEAK QUICKLY FOR EMPHASIS

AND THIS IS HOW YOU SAY "THIS DESSERT LOOKS SO DELICIOUS, IT IS ACTUALLY DESTROYING MY MIND""

SSSUUUGGOOI!!!!

extended   keep going!

hey, guess what? I found out my mom bought that spider-man sweater because it reminded her of you when you freaked out from excitement over the spider-man ride at Universal Studios!

WHAT?!

um... kind of like now

SUGOI!! SUGOI!! SUGOI!! SUGOI!!

← the "repeated sugoi"

[end]
2014 damian

now that you know this word, there are probably only 3 or 4 more that you need to learn before you can fake your way through numerous conversations!

Next stop was Hokkaido, Japan's second largest Island. If Japan is a "j", Hokkaido is the "dot"

hokkaido

TAKOYAKI

simplified map to show the "j"

welcome to apan!

← Look at real map for accuracy

First stop in Hokkaido was the small ski village Niseko - where the official language is Australian

g'day - mate!

hey, where are all the Japanese People?

STEPCHILD

20ft snow drifts

We stayed at a traditional hotel (ryokan), which consists of a small room that transforms

shower on sen

table

← table

day

table is moved and futons are rolled out to sleep

night

↑ TATAMI MATS

It also had a small natural hot spring bath (onsen) connected to the room

HOT! HOT!

COLD! COLD!

towel

the water

the open window Air to ski Hill ...BRRR!

unclosable

After Niseko, we visited the beautiful capital city - Sapporo

KOI SLEEPING IN THE STREAM DOWNTOWN

...and the Sapporo Beer Museum. My favourite parts were the huge collection of vintage ads, and flavoured ice creams after the tour...

crowd cheering the Giant elephant

1910

CLASSIC

KAI?? KURI

BEER SAMPLES

SALT + PEPPER

PUMPKIN

ICE CREAM

Dinner that night was at a tiny "grandma's home cooking" style restaurant with great food...

natto (fermented soybean)

DAIKON

WASABI

RICE

OKRA

raw egg

TORORO (slimy potato)

Nameko (slimy mushroom)

Hokkaido is well known for its vegetables and dairy farms

hashi- chopsticks

Shortly after, we returned to Canada-where learned 'reflex' bowing continued for several days...

HAI! ARIGATOU!

hi...uh... what?

little bow

end...until next trip!

another great thing about Hokkaido was all of the snow! you can see the sapporo beer museum in the background as well as my slimy and delicious meal!

HOKKAIDO ONSEN   damian 2014

This last drawing is me in the in-room onsen
(steamy background photo) in the hotel (ryokan)
in Niseko.

I drew this one on the flight leaving Hokkaido
and heading back to Tokyo....a couple of the
stewardesses on the flight had some questions
for me when they saw this.

banff, canada

travel sketches

sometimes i leave the cartoon drawing table and
draw things outside - these are those times...

"who's on first?" - calgary, canada

"swan lake"

singapore botanical
gardens.
(ink & watercolour)

"confederation park"

calgary, alberta
(ink & watercolour)

"branching out"

calgary, alberta
(ink & watercolour)

"troll falls"

calgary, alberta
(no actual trolls falling)
(ink & watercolour)

"crane style vs worm style"

i'd like to think i can explain this one...you see, it started out as a sketch of a building but then this huge bus parked blocking my view.. so i started drawing this crane, but then the crane moved and i lost the whole perspective...then i went home and drew the crane with leaking pipes, a ship anchor and a giant worm or it....pretty straightforward, really. (ink & watercolour)

"no dogs allowed in starbucks"

i suspect this dog is not a coffee drinker either... instead, it was tied up outside on a freezing winter day.
(ink & watercolour)

"open for business...but not today"

an interesting & colourful warehouse in inglewood calgary.
(ink & watercolour)

Skully.

by damian willcox

"death defying"

(adobe ideas)

Skully.

by damian willcox

"killer dinnerware"

(adobe illustrator)

"bone scan"

featuring my semi recurring "boney-m" character.
(ink & watercolour)

Skully.

by damian willcox

"teed off"

also a page from my sketchbook
capturing the original comic idea...
(adobe illustrator)

Skully.

by damian willcox

"dark alley"

(adobe illustrator)

Skully.

by damian willcox

"a poultry matter"

(adobe illustrator)

Skully.

by damian willcox

"seasick"

notice how the cat's left eye is his 'skully' eye?
this will become vitally important in the near future!
(adobe illustrator)

Skully.

by damian willcox

"bungle gym"

(adobe illustrator)

"skully kitty"

i have drawn a whole story about how skully kitty lost an eye, and i STILL get it wrong...it should be the left eye (skully kitty's, not yours) as seen to the right.
(ink & watercolour)

"remembrance"

(ink & watercolour)

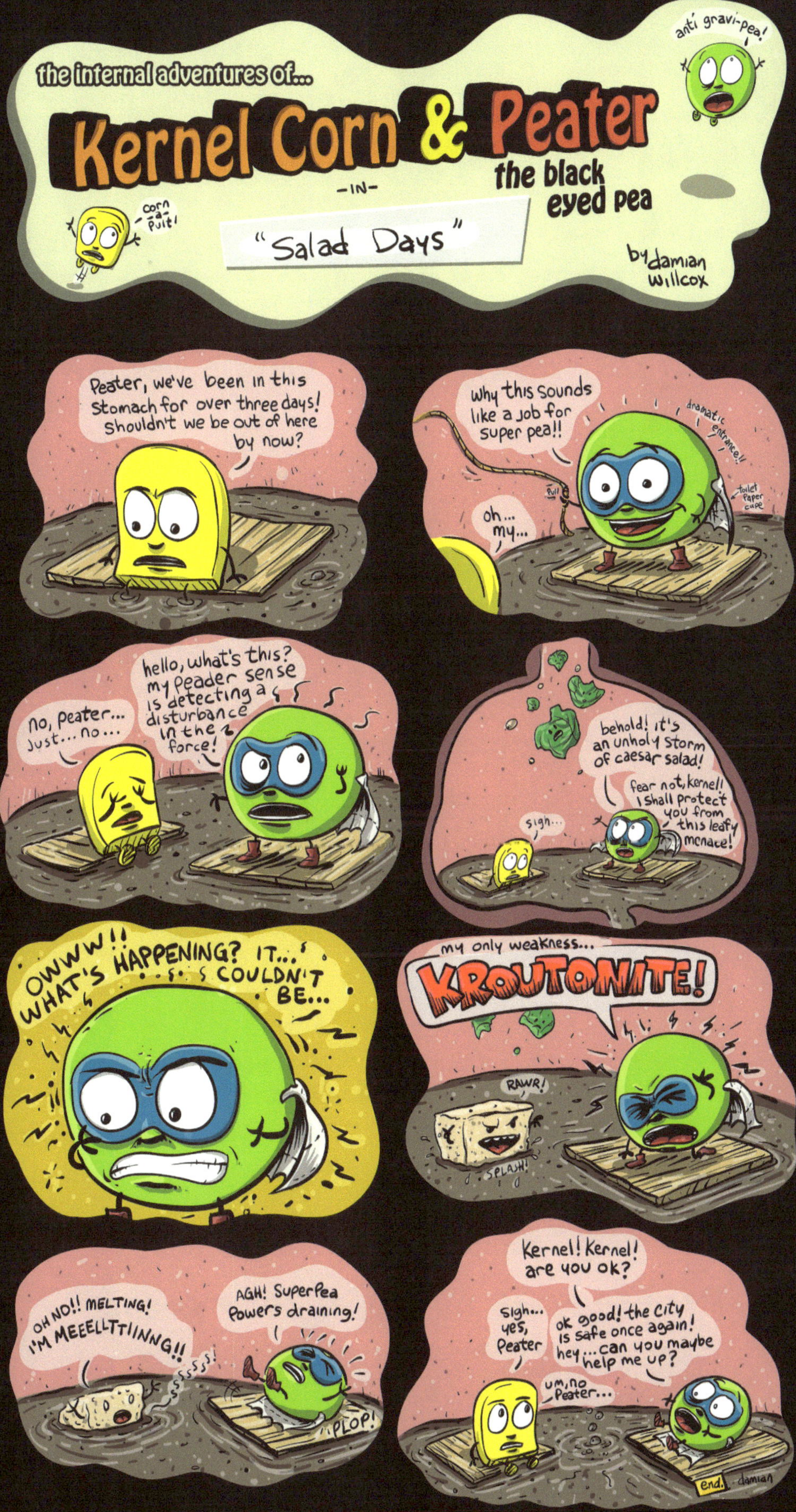

the internal adventures of...
Kernel Corn & Peater
-IN-
the black eyed pea
corn-a-pult!
anti gravi-pea!
"Salad Days"
by damian willcox
Peater, we've been in this stomach for over three days! Shouldn't we be out of here by now?
Why this sounds like a job for super pea!!
dramatic entrance!!
toilet paper cape
oh... my...
hello, what's this? my peader sense is detecting a disturbance in the force!
no, peater... just... no...
behold! it's an unholy storm of caesar salad!
fear not, kernel! I shall protect you from this leafy menace!
sigh...
OWWW!! WHAT'S HAPPENING? IT... COULDN'T BE...
my only weakness...
KROUTONITE!
RAWR!
SPLASH!
OH NO!! MELTING! I'M MEEELLTTIINNG!!
AGH! SuperPea Powers draining!
PLOP!
Kernel! Kernel! are you ok?
sigh... yes, Peater
ok good! the city is safe once again! hey... can you maybe help me up?
um, no Peater...
end. damian

"how to identify bigfoot"

(ink & watercolour)

"inktopus"

(ink & watercolour)

"to seek out new life"

(manga studio)

"the curse of the vinepire"

(adobe ideas)

JERK CHICKEN.

"fowl play"

(adobe ideas)

"EGGS IN THE 1950'S"

"history lesson"

(ink & watercolour)

(you're probably wondering which comic came first...)

"in-bee-ana jones & the lost honeybear shrine"

(ink & watercolour)

"think sweet thoughts"

"IT SAYS I'VE BEEN KNOTTY"

"failed auditions: wolverine"

so...i've always wondered what superhero movies would
be like if i played the lead. ...wonder no more.
(ink & watercolour)

"failed auditions: spider-man"

(ink & watercolour)

"failed auditions: the hulk"

(ink & watercolour)

"ghastly laundromat"

(adobe ideas)

ghost stories

this next section focuses on the best kind of ghosts: the classic ones made up of bedsheets, campy scenarios, wry humour and the best of intentions.

"ghostenstein"

one bedsheet, one classic monster, one blender.
(ink & watercolour)

"sprained an-ghoul"

(ink & watercolour)

"arthritic insomniac ghost"

(ink & watercolour)

"ghostzilla"

(ink & watercolour)

"gourdzilla"

(ink & watercolour)

"gordzilla, legal advisor"

(ink & watercolour)

"spicy lunch"

(manga studio)

GODZINJA damian 2013

"godzinja"

(ink & watercolour)

jetpack

"jetpack bird:
the early years"

(ink & watercolour)

"the maiden voyage"

(ink, watercolour & salt)

bird

"jetpack bird: reporting for duty"

(ink & watercolour)

what started out as an idea that simply amused me (why would a bird need a jetpack?) took on a life of its own...much like my other characters seem to. i'd like to put together a jetpack bird & ninja worm comic sometime, but for now...

"JETPACK BIRD BUYS A LOTTERY TICKET"

"jetpack bird buys a lottery ticket"

(ink & watercolour)

"ninja worm"

and so the diabolical archnemesis to jetpack bird emerges from the depths of the earth! who will win?!
just don't cut him in two, he's good at math, and can multiply just like that!
(ink & watercolour)

NINJA WORM

damian 2018

"ninja worm & the unexpected visitor"

(acrylic gouache on canvas)

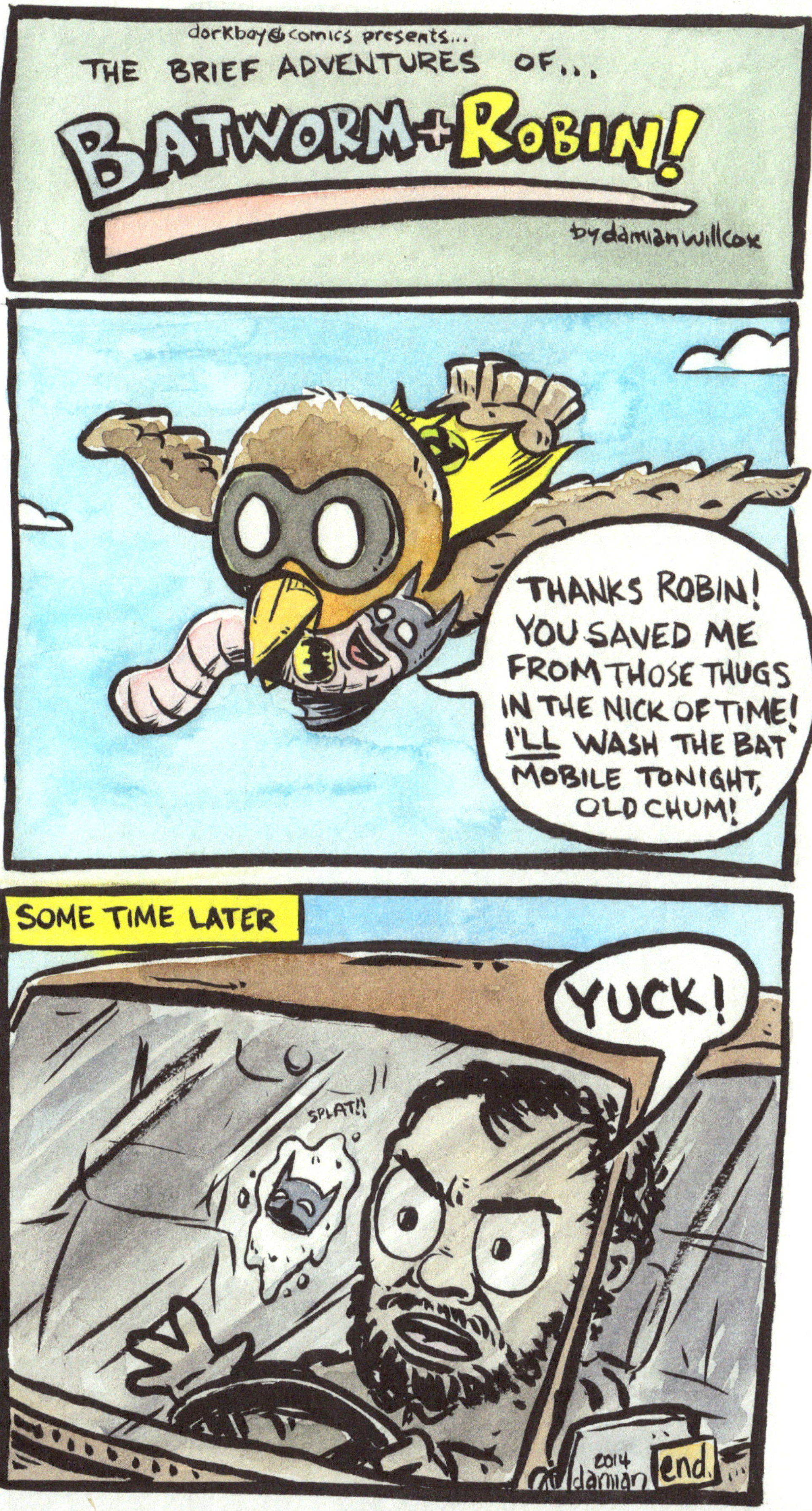
dorkbay comics presents...
THE BRIEF ADVENTURES OF...
BATWORM + ROBIN!
by damian willcox
THANKS ROBIN! YOU SAVED ME FROM THOSE THUGS IN THE NICK OF TIME! I'LL WASH THE BAT MOBILE TONIGHT, OLD CHUM!
SOME TIME LATER
YUCK!
SPLAT!!
2014 damian
end.

"clark's bad news day"

(ink & watercolour)

TRUTH PASTE

damian 2013

"denterrogation"

(ink & watercolour)

and just as quickly as the veggie hotdog had emerged from the water and eaten the plankton, so it disappeared into the depths.

damian 2013

"the legend of the veggie hotdog"

(ink & watercolour)

"fly me to the moon."   damian 2014

"fly me to the moon"

(ink & watercolour)

CRIME DOESN'T PAY, BLAH!
INKTOBER #11
RAWR!!
INKTOBER #12
INKTOBER #13
OCT 1 2013
BUS STOP
INKTOBER #10
toast ghost
EGADS!
"EGADSZILLA"
blah!
IF SPACE IS THE FINAL FRONTIER, SHOULDN'T IT BE CALLED THE "BACK TIER"?
INKTOBER #20
I am the molar of the story, yes?
whirr
INKTOBER #18
INKTOBER #16
"I'M ACTUALLY THE TALL ONE IN THE FAMILY"
KORN DRACULA!
BLAH!
INKTOBER #29
VAMPEATER!
blah!
INKTOBER #30
blah!
INKTOBER #31 "VAMPIRE CAT"
INKTOBER #22 "BASS SOLO"
EXACT CHANGE OOOOOOOOONLY!
INKTOBER #28 "VAMPIRE TAT"
blah!
INKTOBER #23 "PUMPKINHEAD"
BLAH! WHICH WAY TO THE BLOOD BANK?
"VAMPIRE BAT" INKTOBER #26
"VAMPIRE MAT" INKTOBER #27

inktober!

some guy invented 'inktober'. i took part this year.

the rules are as follows:
1. draw everyday in october
2. refer to october as inktober
3. don't talk about inkclub

"if i made the movie 'pacific rim'"

it would be pretty much just like this...
(ink & watercolour)

"where maple syrup comes from"

this was a suggestion from my wife...she's much funnier than i am, but it also proves that i'm not the only morbid one.
(ink & watercolour)

"the girl without a pearl earring"
(adobe ideas)

"danger ahead agent 17, but we have the utmost faith in you"
(adobe ideas)

"summer"
(adobe ideas)

"clark's new contacts"
(ink & watercolour)

(the frightening tale of Dr. Jekyll and Mr. Hide-and-go-seek)

"alter ego"
(ink & watercolour)

"what do you sell to a salesman?"
(ink & watercolour)

"super onigiri"
(adobe ideas)

"flying peas corps"
(adobe ideas)

"striking resemblance"

(ink & watercolour)

"captain blackbear(d)"
(ink & watercolour)

about the artist...

damian willcox is an award nominated cartoonist
that has been publishing his comics and artwork both
in print and online for almost twenty years.

During that time he has also written the Too Much Coffee Man Opera
with Shannon Wheeler, survived his comics getting TV series related
interest from Hollywood types, and has even appeared in a National
Chinese television show as a 'wealthy foreigner'.

He currently lives in Calgary, Alberta, Canada and spends his days with
his wonderful wife Miyuki and nutty dogs Lychee & Kiwi ("the fruits").

thank you so much for picking up this book - it's a lot of work,
but it really is a labour of love for me, and i can't seem to stop.
i hope you enjoy the comics as much as i enjoy making them.
thanks again.
your comic friend,

♥damian

damian@dorkboycomics.com
www.dorkboycomics.com

twitter @dorkboycomics
facebook facebook.com/damiandraws
google+ plus.dorkboycomics.com
tumblr dorkboycomics.tumblr.com

HOW IT FEELS WHEN I DRAW.

it's been sweet - see you soon,

♥damian

www.ingramcontent.com/pod-product-compliance
Lightning Source LLC
Chambersburg PA
CBHW061356090426
42739CB00003B/42